THE DEATH OF COCK ROBIN

THE DEATH OF COCK ROBIN

Poems by W. D. Snodgrass

Paintings by DeLoss McGraw

Afterword by William Chace

NEWARK: UNIVERSITY OF DELAWARE PRESS
LONDON AND TORONTO: ASSOCIATED UNIVERSITY PRESSES

Associated University Presses
440 Forsgate Drive
Cranbury, NJ 08512

Associated University Presses
25 Sicilian Avenue
London WC1A 2QH, England

Associated University Presses
2133 Royal Windsor Drive
Unit 1
Mississauga, Ontario
Canada L5J 1K5

The paper used in this publication meets the requirements
of the American National Standard for Permanence of Paper
for Printed Library Materials Z39.48-1984.

Library of Congress Cataloging-in-Publication Data

Snodgrass, W. D. (William De Witt), 1926–
  The death of Cock Robin.

  1. Cock Robin (Fictitious character)—Poetry.
2. Birds—Poetry. I. McGraw, DeLoss. . II. Title.
PS3537.N32D4 1989   811'.54   85-41050
ISBN 0-87413-304-1 (alk. paper)

Printed in R.O.C.

For Michelle, Curtis, Holland and Dylan

Acknowledgments

The following poems first appeared in the publications indicated; thanks is due the editors of those publications for permission to reprint and for transferral of copyright.

The Kenyon Review, Spring 1985:
   "The Charges against Cock Robin," "Call for Clues" and "Auction."

The New York Quarterly, Summer and Fall, 1985:
   "W. D. Picks a Bouquet for Cock Robin but Cannot Separate the Thorns from the Flowers," "W. D. Searches for Cock Robin in the Weave of his Thought," "Cock Robin Takes Refuge in the Storm House," "W. D. Becomes Entangled in the Nest of His Thought" and "Storm Family's Anthem."

Salmagundi, Summer, 1985:
   "Interrogation," "W. D. Finds Cock Robin," "W. D. Creates a Device for Escaping," "Disguised as Cock Robin, W. D. Escapes" and "W. D. Disguised as Cock Robin and Hidden Deep in Crimson."

Negative Capability, Fall, 1985:
   "W. D. Creates a Device for Inverting Mr. Evil," "W. D., Don't Fear that Animal," "W. D. Meets Mr. Evil while Removing the Record of Bartok and Replacing it with a Recent Recording by the Everly Brothers in Order to Create a Mood Conducive to Searching for Cock Robin," "W. D. is Concerned about the Character Assassination of Cock Robin," "Credo" and "W. D. Attempts to Save Cock Robin."

Word and Image, January–March, 1986:
   "W. D. Assists in Supporting Cock Robin's Roost" and "Cock Robin's Roost Protects W. D. from Mr. Evil."

Light Year '87:
   "W. D., Don't Fear that Animal," "Credo," "Coroner's Inquest," and "The Poet Ridiculed by Hysterical Academics."

Graham House Review, January, 1987:
   "W. D. Lifts Ten Times the Weight of His Own Body."

The American Poetry Review, January/February, 1987:
   "W. D. Tries to Warn Cock Robin," "Lullaby: The Comforting of Cock Robin," "W. D. Consults with Kafka and Dostoevsky Concerning the Whereabouts of Cock Robin," "W. D. and Cock Robin Discuss the Dreaded Interrogation," "W. D. Sits in Kafka's Chair and Is Interrogated Concerning the Assumed Death of Cock Robin" and "Assuming Fine Feathers, W. D. Takes Flight."

W. D. Snodgrass wishes to express gratitude to the Corporation of Yaddo and the Virginia Center for the Creative Arts for periods spent in residence.

Contents

THE DEATH OF COCK ROBIN

W. D. Picks a Bouquet for Cock Robin . . .   60 × 40 in.

W. D. Picks a Bouquet for Cock Robin but Cannot
Separate the Thorns from the Flowers

I found myself intent
To find profusions of rare bloom,
Harvesting armfuls that should scent
And ornament your room.

Or failing that, some floral
Cordon summer might bequeathe,
Or weave some ivy or live laurel's
Coronal and wreathe.

Yet all my season's rambles
Seeing I found nowhere to pick it
But in the flourishing, keen brambles
Of my brain's ingrown thicket

Accept, then, this small vase
Of blossom, thistleflower and thorn
To lend some honor to the place
You rest, or to be worn.

The Charges against Cock Robin

Speaker: His Honor James T. "Just
   call me Jim" Crowe.
Chorus: Titmouse and Dormouse, Eagle
   and Seagull, Cuckoo and Water Shrew.

It is charged he's been known to warble
                    (Deplorable!)
An aria, a love song, or recitatif
                    (Good Grief!)
When he goes walking, long after curfew
                    (Lord preserve you!)
Waking up both town and country.
                    (What effrontery!)

We find it far more injurious
                    (We're just furious!)
That he sings beyond other birds' range
                    (He's strange!)
Though they practice and pay the best teachers
                    (Poor creatures!)
While his tunes baffle us and defeat us.
                    (Elitist!)

Moreover, he dresses in a fashion
                    (Far too dashing!)
Neither generic nor respectable—
                    (Get expectable!)
All sorts of bright shreds and patches
                    (Nothing matches!)
That make no more sense than cuneiform.
                    (Get a uniform!)

If one wishes to sound operatic
                    (We're emphatic!)

The Poet Ridiculed by Hysterical Academics   22 × 30 in.

Or to break forth with a cantata

       (All birds oughta)

Always be careful to bring along

       (Like a singalong)

Fitting clothes and a high-sounding moral.

       (Get oral; get choral; wax
                floral!)

He is urged by us birds of one stripe

       (Be our type!)

And enjoined by us cats of one color:

       (Get duller!)

Be a horse of one congruous feather.

       (All together!)

Cease these lyrics of lust, rum and riot
(Keep it quiet!)
And incitements to profligate violence.
(Silence!)

W. D., Don't Fear That Animal

My hat leaps up when I behold
  A rhino in the sky;
When crocodiles upon the wing
Perch on my windowsill to sing,
All my loose ends turn blue and cold;
  I don't know why.

W. D., Don't Fear That Animal   22 × 30 in.

My knuckles whiten should I hark
    Some lonely python's cry;
Should a migrating wedge of moose
Honk, it can shake my molars loose—
Or when, at heaven's gate, the shark
        Doth pine and sigh.

My socks may slide off at the sight
    Of giant squids on high
Or baby scorpions bubbling up
Inside my morning coffee cup—
Somehow, it spoils my appetite;
        My throat gets dry.

At dawn, I lift my gaze in air
    Cock Robin to espy
And mark instead some bright-eyed grizzly;
The hairs back of my neck turn bristly.
That's foolish since we know that they're
        More scared than I.

Such innocent creatures mean no harm;
    They wouldn't hurt a fly.
Still, when I find myself between a
Playful assembly of hyena,
I can't help feeling some alarm;
        I've got to try.

W. D. Lifts Ten Times the Weight of His Own Body

1.

These Russian heavies are all wrong
On force and form. No doubt they're strong
But if you turn into a hulk
Of mass and muscle, your own bulk

W. D. Lifts Ten Times the Weight . . .   41 × 30 in.

Can drop you into a deep oxtrap:
You lift yourself by your own jockstrap
Besides those weights you jerk and press;
So it's essential to weigh less,
Embodying uplift and *ballon.*
The way these Russians put weight on
You'd think it's going out of style. It's gone.

One lad I knew hefted a heifer
Daily; it grew light as a zephyr
Even when swollen to its full
Beefy bloatitude as a bull.
Myself, I uphold every day
The selfsame load, but meanwhile weigh
Less than I did the day before.
Like ants, I now tote ten times more
Than my own tonnage. At the gym
I pare myself down, airier, slim,
Till I become a 98–
Pound Charles, at last, of underweight.
An auto-heist, combatting gravity,
I rise up in high spirits and levity,
Unbending my irreverent knee
To overcome brute force and mightiness;
Getting things off the ground takes flightiness.

2.

Snodgrass's Second Theorem states: You're
Stronger when bending to things' nature.
Don't lift; release things toward the skies—
Release what's meant, or means, to rise.
Raise jackstraws, piles of pickup sticks,
Spokes, pikes and pickets, spikes, toothpicks;
Raise kite sticks, stalks, struts, Roman candles,
Rays of bright sunlight, hafts, helves, handles;
Raise vaulters' poles, Olympic javelin
Shafts, sword strokes, streaks of starlight travelling
Through black wastes; raise up jet trails, tracers;
Raise fish rods, bike spokes, lances, lasers.
Be one with all things light and luminous
Like a Zen sage or some old Humanist
Whose drive to transport and to heighten meant
Shouldering a general Enlightenment.
Then, like a Chinese waiter, scoop
This universal mare's nest soup
To shoulder level, all the while
A fat moon peering through the pile
And cosmic tangle has to smile

To see Cock Robin, calm, at rest
And sleeping sound in that vast nest
Or twiggy burden, borne along
The steady airstream on a strong
Dream's wingbeat or on springs of song.

Lullaby:
The Comforting of Cock Robin

Smooth quill and bristle down;
Soothe day's shrill whistle down;
Bestow the head
To its own bed
Of soft moss and thistledown.

May the insatiable powers,
    The vast cravings of the dark,
Spend their forces and their hours
    Each on each, or miss their mark.

May the raccoon and the agile
    Long-tailed, long-toothed squirrel pass,
Find the fox and miss the fragile
    Clutch of eggs in the long grass.

May the weasel, the lithe snake,
    May the housecat on the prowl,
Creeping up the limbs all night,
    Meet and satisfy the owl.

Let the shivering eyelid close,
    The down-surrounded egg turn in
On the steady urge that grows
    What might be from what has been

Till beneath the illusory lamps,
    Burned out, the hankering moth miller
Sprawls, and toward fresh new green leaves tramps
    The lockstep, workday caterpillar

While, fresh, the sprinkler on the lawn
    Lures the young, nutritious worm
To loll and sunbathe in the dawn,
    Plump, seductive, pink and firm.

Then shall your well-supported song,
    Drafting the full breath's thermal currents,
Carry the mastered woodlands, strong
    With portamento, with endurance.

> Smooth quill and bristle down;
> Soothe day's shrill whistle down;
> Bestow the head
> To its own bed
> Of soft moss and thistledown.

W. D. Is Concerned about the Character Assassination of Cock Robin

> *Yo no quiero verla;*
> *Yo no lo se.*

Come, Rosie Angel, clasp
    Over each eye, each ear,
Your gauze-soft hands that grasp
    What not to see or hear.

> Don't care to,
> Won't dare to,
> Can't bear to
> See.

Lullaby: The Comforting of Cock Robin   30 × 22 in.

Should the secret inspectors
    Knock once at your locked door,
Not even bill collectors
    Know your name any more.

                        Don't choose to,
                        Refuse to,
                        No use to
                                Hear.

As your stock falls, old friends
    Fall off. Fall into danger—
If you survive depends
    On some total stranger.

                        Past all thought;
                        Best forgot,
                        Surely not
                                Here.

Small wonder dear friends turn
    Acrimonious and cruel
When Love's most fierce fires burn
    Denatured hate for fuel.

                        Never more,
                        Neither nor,
                        Not friend or
                                Foe.

All you once knew goes strange.
    Some you've known all their lives
Outside your window range,
    Tongues flashing slick as knives

                        Numb, deaf, blind;
                        May we find
                        No man's mind
                                So.

W. D. Is Concerned about the Character Assassination . . .   30 × 22 in.

Where Cock Robin's once-loved name
   Sank like fat in the sands
And his good neighbors came
   Licking their snouts and hands.

                  I'd deceive
                  All who'd grieve.
                  Come; believe
                        Me.

A face, now, fixed with wide
   Open eyes, constantly
Loitering near outside,
   Keeps close watch over me.

                  No, never;
                  Nerves, sever;
                  Don't ever
                        Know.

                              Yo no quiero verla;
                              Yo no lo se.

W. D. Tries to Warn Cock Robin

The Brutish are coming, the Brutish;
The Rude-Coats with snares and bum-drumming!
      The Skittish and Prudish
      The Brattish and Crude
      Who'll check on your morals
      And find your song's lewd
Then strip off the bay leaves and laurels
That garnished your brows and your food.
All tongues and all tastebuds benumbing,

W. D. Tries to Warn Cock Robin

22 × 30 in.

They'll dull all your senses
Then lull your defenses
And rule you through blue-nosed and tasteless pretenses:
The Brutish!

The Ruffians are coming, the Ruffians!
Those rowdies with mandolins strumming!

They'll stomp out your stuffings
And all you've been taught;
　　　Pan-Slobs from Vulgaria
　　　Will come; if you're caught
Knowing more than your own name, they'll bury you.
Inter your own brain, so they'll not
Take more than your watch and your plumbing.
　　　Those red-necked invaders,
　　　Those radical raiders,
Who'll root out free thinkers, free lovers, free traders!
　　　　　　The Ruffians!

The Merkans are coming, the Merkans!
Those jingoes whose jingles keep gumming
　　　Your intimate workings
　　　With terms periphrastic;
　　　The fare that they offer
　　　Will ruin your gastric
Intestinal tract; then they'll cover
Your country with asphalt and plastic
To hide what keeps oozing and scumming.
　　　They'll plug up your juices,
　　　Slipcover your sluices,
Then turn your equipment to mercantile uses:
　　　　　　The Merkans!

The Krishans are coming, the Krishans!
Hear the chants, psalms and hymns they keep humming!
　　　They'll offer you visions
　　　Of undying blisses
　　　With premises, promises,
　　　And crucifixes
To prop up all Questioning Thomases.
They'll double criss-cross you with kisses
And blessings. With grim mimes and mumming,
　　　The hairy one omming,
　　　The balded ones psalming,
　　　With rituals and riddles

And charity victuals,
You'll jump into hellfire to get off their griddle,
            The Krishans!

The Youmans are coming, the Youmans!
Hear the backslapping rascals, the chumming
            Of Masculs and Woomans
            Who built up this Babel
            Of Atoms and Evils
            And hope that they're able
To raise some more cain and upheaval.
That Garden foreclosed in the fable
Foretold how this world's going slumming:
            In cold greed, the cowards
            Still split and unite
            For unneeded powers,
            While backbiting spite
Pulls down all their towers;
            With air, sea and soil
            And their own minds to spoil
And spin their bright cosmos to unending night,
            The Youmans!

Cock Robin Takes Refuge in the Storm House

The sky's unsettled; hawk-winged shadows
Swoop overhead all day long, scrawling
Their logo on the tarnished meadows.
Blood-bright, a leaf reeled past me, falling.
Did I hear my storm family calling?

And no bird sings. These weeds keep bristling.
A chill wind hisses at my ear
Trying to tell me something, whistling
Like a consistent, heart-felt jeer.
They don't live all that far from here.

Cock Robin Takes Refuge in the Storm House   22 × 30 in.

Like trains colliding, or deep thunder,
I heard a heavy tree-trunk buckle,
Crack in the green woods and go under.
From someplace else, a greasy chuckle.
They'll need a fourth to play pinochle.

I don't mean to alarm you, but
The trees keep nodding like a jury
Whose minds are satisfied and shut;
No doubt we'll just get a light flurry.
Still, it's not nice to let them worry.

If they don't hear every so often
You know your storm mother gets nervous—
She'll think you're sick, maimed, in your coffin,
Abandoned somewhere—Lord preserve us,
Why, I'd be doing them a service!

The whole air's gone a doubtful color
Like milk gone blenky, like children chided.
I'll take some sweet rolls or a cruller,
See that they're snug and well-provided.
Who'd check up on them unless I did?

Storm Family's Anthem

—For Curt and Carole, Bill and Rose,
   Dick and Takako, Phil and Juanita,
   Myreen, Judy, Gary.

When the sky's all crazed with lightning
While the clouds roll black and frightening
   Like the world's started smouldering somewhere
And a huge old thunderboomer
Sounds its guns, come be our roomer
   On the back of an old kitchen chair.
When a schoolbus or a dumptruck swerves
Like Dodgem cars on highway curves
   While gasps, shouts and shrieks fill the air,
If your car spins like Pavlova did,
You're safer on our sofa-bed
   Upheld by an old kitchen chair.
      And we swear
      We'll be there
   When the rain, snow and sleet fill the air,
      Where we'll share

Simple fare
On the back of an old kitchen chair.

When ice keeps caking the windshield
So snowplows wander through a field
   And can't find the road anywhere,
While drivers wade from what they drove,
We'll just throw something on the stove
   And warm up this old kitchen chair.
While the roads fill with abandoned cars,
We've got sweet pickles canned in jars,
   Tomatoes and peach jam or pear.
Let the Ski-Doos drive out, having sport;
You just come ride our davenport
   Founded fast on an old kitchen chair.
     Tough as birch,
     Though we lurch
   When the storm winds come battering the air,
     We can perch
     Calm as church
   On the crest of an old kitchen chair.

When the faultlines shift, a major quake
Makes public buildings squirm and shake
   And gaps in the dam make you stare;
If the bridge sways and you rock a lot,
Come over for hot chocolate
   Plunked down on an old kitchen chair.
While the gales tear up old, settled oaks
That fall on roofs and passing folks,
   While wires, shooting sparks, fill the air,
If the powercrews can't handle it,
We always keep a candle lit
   Aglow on an old kitchen chair.
     When a scare
     Or despair,
   S.O.S. and distress fill the air,

Cock Robin Consults with His Storm Family

22 × 30 in.

Still we dare
Light a flare
Standing fast on an old kitchen chair.

When the clouds spout like a faucet,
Hang your raingear in our closet
    While we wrench out your drenched underwear;
Then, like flapping flags, your socks can fly—
Come on up, keep your ankles dry
    Aloft on an old kitchen chair.
While we open cans of kippers
Get a hot bath, find some slippers
    And a blanket; we won't leave you bare;

But we'll leave your shoes ooze sloppily—
It's time for some Monopoly
    Dealt out on an old kitchen chair.
      Through the drear
      Atmosphere
    While the fog, mist and murk fill the air,
      Give a cheer—
      We'll appear,
    Calm and clear on our old kitchen chair.

We won't question your opinions
While you roost in our dominions;
    They're your own and we simply don't care.
We won't ask you what your father does
'Cause things like that don't bother us
    On the heights of an old kitchen chair.
If your folks are influential
That won't serve as a credential;
    If your forebears are known, just forbear.
Even though you're high and mighty,
We'll still offer you a nightie
Off the back of an old kitchen chair.
      When the bear
      Seeks his lair,
While upheaval and need fill the air,
      We'll prepare
      Meals to spare
And a berth on our old kitchen chair.

We don't have much charm and brilliance
And we won't make multimillions;
    We're behind times and quite unaware;
Yet we've learned some minor talents—
The resilience and the balance
    To latch on to an old kitchen chair.
As we see the whole thing, high ideals
Mean: Keep your head above your heels

Like clowns on a wire at the fair.
So while hostile forces struggle
Snuggle in here where we juggle
   On our toes on an old kitchen chair.
     Just beware
     Since it's rare
   To stay level, upright, head in air;
     Though we're square,
     It takes flair
   And the poise for an old kitchen chair.

All your fancier emotions
Fall someplace outside our notions;
   We can't stop you from tearing your hair
With depressions, griefs and worries,
But in case of thick snowflurries
   Just resort to the old kitchen chair.
We can't drive away your inner storm
But we'll keep your bed and dinner warm
   And help talk away a nightmare;
So in case you get a weeping jag
Come creep inside our sleeping bag
   Tucked up on an old kitchen chair.
     Milk that's spilt,
     Blame and guilt
   And a cold sense of wrong in the air
     Sometimes wilt
     In a quilt
   Wrapped up snug on an old kitchen chair.

We'll all turn the dial together
Tuning in some better weather;
   While we wait for the news to declare
That the world's got back together,
Preen and check each tattered feather
   For repair on that old kitchen chair.
Once the air's filled up with zephyrs
And the fields with lambs and heifers
   While birdsong and bees throng the air,

Then go out and get your snootie full
Of landscapes bright and beautiful,
    Launched straight from that old kitchen chair.
        Still we'll stare
        Through the fair
    Sunny days and the flower-swarming air,
        'Cause we care
        How you fare
    Forth so far from our old kitchen chair.

W. D. Searches for Cock Robin in the Weave of His Thought

when i set out thistle
seed for finches, i
got thistles, then let
blackcaps and thimbleberries
use up the hayfield's
old manure, let hawthorn and
chokecherry overtop
the rotting orchard.
all song, no doubt, demands
some wilderness, a little
wholesome waste—a
shrike, no doubt, might like
these thorns, bunting or wren
roost in among these prickles.
fishflesh, no doubt, is
prosy lacking fish
bones; frost flowers
bristle; even stars
shoot spiny rays. this
is ridiculous. suppose
all heaven's winged choirs

flew in to rest, nest and roost
and spun out all their music
while i had roger tory peterson
by heart, i couldn't see
a bird or tell his song.

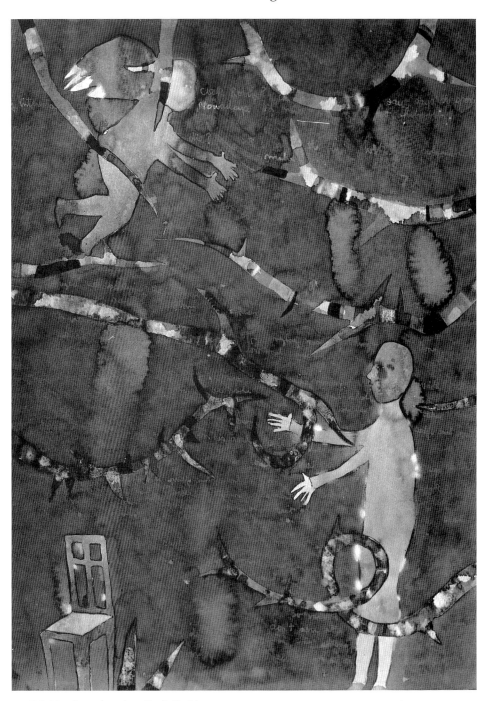

W. D. Searches for Cock Robin . . .   30 × 22 in.

W. D. Assists in Supporting Cock Robin's Roost

the
roof-
peak with
its hornets &
the grackle's nest;
the eavesboards squirrels
squirm through into the attic
then gnaw at the windowsills;
this back wall with blistered
shingles where these bats get
in and nest; these baseboards
that hide, eight inches deep,
years of dead flies and dried
grain kernels field mice once
hid there, not to speak about
those holes that let weasels,
muskrats and even young wood-
chucks pass through the walls
—til the whole neighborhood,
til everyone except the owner
lived in here—has got to go.
replace it all. for now, tho,
we can just prop the lee side
using this old thorny branch,
so; then wedge another branch
against the right—our effect
is not wholly thus unlike the
swooping & far-elbowed flying
buttresses we note in certain
french cathedrals dating from
the gothic period—surely, no
one would ever notice, maybe,
that this 8-storey bird house
stands, or 8-bird story house
was
founded
on a small
round
ball

•

W. D. Assists in Supporting Cock Robin's Roost 30 × 22 in.

W. D. Becomes Entangled in the Nest of His Thought

it is a rank, unweeded
veritable Africa where you
run guns or seek
unfathomable riches, some
funhouse, barbershop, some Versailles
Hall of Mirrors where
each thought invokes its
counterthought, each
desire its
antipathy, where all is
double and that double
doubled, these tendrils inter-
woven to the heaven's
immensity while

W. D. Becomes Entangled in the Nest of His Thought   22 × 30 in.

cherubim (red) and
seraphim (blue), these
αγγελος and δαίμονες, lithe
goldfish swimming in a bowl,
slip through the boughs and branches
as though veins and arteries
could be the messengers of . . . . but
where did i begin? . . . . until
you meet your own self
coming out the other side and,
unsure of welcome, hold
your hand out to inquire:
Cock Robin, i presume?

W. D. Consults with Kafka and Dostoevski Concerning the Whereabouts of Cock Robin

D. Go straight to prison; don't pass Go;
        Claim that you're just a visitor.
    No doubt you'll find him in there, though
        Disguised as an Inquisitor.

K. Prowl the worst dives; no doubt he's passing
        For some cutthroat or mob "torpedo";
        What more ingenious incognito
    Than going masked as your own assassin?

D. Announce rewards—dead or alive—
        For knowledge of his whereabouts;
    Curiosity, or some such drive,
        Will keep him snooping thereabouts.

K. Ah no; we want his sense of sin to rest;
        He'll hide out if he's being traced.
        Have large NOT WANTED posters placed
    On billboards; say you've lost all interest.

W. D. Consults with Kafka and Dostoevski . . .   22 × 30 in.

   D. Wrong; wrong; play on his sense of guilt.
        Say: Law can't serve its purpose—
    Full restitution of blood spilt—
        Till he brings in his corpus.

   K. Wait; he'll come seek us, once he's shriven
        Of every fault and deep transgression.
        Say this: Just sign a full confession
    That you've been killed, then all's forgiven.

W. D. Meets Mr. Evil While Removing the Record of Bartok and Replacing it with a Recent Recording by the Everly Brothers in Order to Create a Mood Conducive to Searching for Cock Robin

So; caught you in, my fine young fellow?
Though I'd just drop past to say Hello,
Dish out some hot poop—how to find
The outlawed Redbreast on your mind:
His Cockiness whose Robinhood
Echoes the Forest of Sure Would.

I know *you*, though. Just call me Mystery
Bill, B.S., M.S. in doctored History,
Onetime Sheriff of Nothing Am,
Ambassador of Havasham,

W. D. Meets Mr. Evil . . .   40 × 60 in.

Last Past Master of Hoke Lodge,
High Priest and Medium for Mirage.

First off, we've got to change the record—
Such grim sounds evidence a checkered
Past—then concoct an atmosphere full
Of hopeful tunes, loving and cheerful.
Dump these sour tones, this cleverly infernal
Dissonance; we'll choir forth an Everly eternal

Psalm of unchanging Brotherhood,
Fake chords real folks would like real good,
Cut platters of pattering platitudes
To impart the politic, pat attitudes
Taught by our founder, Dr. Garbles,
Who struck dumb multitudes with marbles

Held in mouthfuls of popular melody.
Or better still, this high fidelity
Digital of an eighteen-minute
Gap: you'll feel, each time you spin it,
Pure as a Quaker, freed from violence
And expletives by blissful silence.

To lure down this bird you desire
We'll mute our loot, moot every liar,
Ban all Anacreonisms or Sapphics
Then chart this on our phoni-Graphics,
Banish gloom, gravity and art talk.
Besides, we'll lie about the Bartok.

W. D. Assists in the Protection of Cock Robin's Roost

When the heavens fill with orgies and revels,
Where laser-red angels and shock-blue devils
Scramble to dogfight and clash, helter-skelter,
                    In the world's wreck and welter
                    I'll warden your shelter.

If your whole firmament's invaded at once
By high pressure systems and low pressure fronts,
While hot and cold air masses deadlock in storm,
                    Here under my form
                    Bivouac, dry and warm.

Suppose your whole nature splits in confusion
Of theories, beliefs, moods, and the profusion
Of goods and evils seems one vast delusion,
                    Take time to regroup;
                    I'll cover your coop.

Should some volcanic rage take sudden possession
Of muscles and nerves, yet a vice-like depression
Has clamped down till catatonic compression
                    Paralyzes all forces, then
                    Like trained, camouflage men
                    Or some broad mother hen
                    I'll slipcover your den,
                    Shield your brood, roost and pen
                    Till your song spires again.
                        Say where and when.

W. D. Assists in the Protection of Cock Robin's Roost   22 × 30 in.

Cock
Robin's
Roost
Protects
W. D.   From   Mr. Evil

                                    Come to my arms, my fine young friend;
                                    Overcome this cold resistence; we
                                    Can't bring our differences to an end
                                    Keeping our grounds so distantly.

        May this spell hold us as we **R,**
      This ring of force we're parted by— **O**
        Impassable, firm-fixed and far **B**
            Twixt the likes of you and **I.**
                                    No doubt I'm not so very handsome;
                                    Some judge by one's appearance, so
                                    Many a man condemns me, and some
                                    Are far more like me than they know.

          May this light house's N R **G**
      Reveal your features bright as day; **I**
          Trust by this gleam men may **C**
              No Real Good in you for **A.**
                                    Light cast out on the faults of others
                                    Blinds men to their own faults. We
                                    Also share drives, all men being brothers;
                                    Relinquish this proud enmity.

            Our blood alliance shall be **R**
          True shame, a defect in the **I**
        Your double-cross-eyed poli— **C**
        Would dwindle and waste D O **A.**
                                    Drop such d-fences; we'll double you, De.
              Only across Styx, Mr. **E.**

48

Cock Robin's Roost . . .   30 × 22 in.

W. D. Creates a Device for Inverting Mr. Evil

Swing past, Miss Treavle, swing right by,
Hanging head-downward from the sky;
As worms squirm down threads out of trees
Or clowns dangle from some trapeze
Laced into long gowns, tightly skirted,
So I suspend you here, inverted,
By holding up this hula hoop
You can't leap through, so, *allez-oop,*
Your words get slamdunked, codified,
Scrambled and then transmogrified.
Now, though you mouth me all things EVIL,
I hear them through this medieval
Antenna that receives what's VILE
But transubstantiates its style,

W. D. Creates a Device . . .   22 × 30 in.

Sifting it through this sieve or VEIL
Till all your meanest meanings fail
And your commandments merely give
Me one imperative verb: LIVE.

W. D. Finds Cock Robin

e-good-gad, marquis, my favorite
charade tableau: mary's dive-
bomb dove cracks up or is it
banners in the dust? something to

W. D. Finds Cock Robin   22 × 30 in.

elicit condoling droplets in the
sternest eye. what is this, an
exploded sofa bolster? i wouldn't
touch that thing with ice
tongs. why don't we lug the guts
up on the curbside; we wouldn't
want to gum up someone's axles.
yes, yes — my one big chance for
prime time: paramedic to
the aviary. do you know the fee
for bringing birds in out of
quarantine and tell it to knock
off that wheezing sound. i
haven't got a freezer full of worms:
i could get sued for busted
plumes; malpractice; where do the
doctors live and i don't know the
language. also that
squirming on the ground. i've had
a bad back lately and the village
is 2000 cubits. just help me
heist this bleeder over my
left shoulder, here, i'll
show you how i couldn't
carry it . . .

Call for Clues

Okay, you leaves up there, come clean;
Your turn to sing out: whattaya seen?
You can't just perch there high and mighty
Whispering, rubbing your palms politely.
Speak up; someday you gotta tumble

Down in the dirt, red-faced and humble
Just like him. Now, who done this bird?
Whattaya seen and whattaya heard?

Cough it up, clouds; you're on the hook.
Don't give me no vague, wandering look.
Maybe you're short on shape and "It-ness";
We know damn well you was a witness.
You took in loads; you been aroun';
It weighs on you; it's a bringdown
Holding back. Spill it all, posthaste:
Who brung that bird out here to waste?

Okay, you stars, you sun and moon,
Pipe up; we're here to cop your tune.
You gone past here, so come acrost.
You gonna let his tunes get lost,
Buried in self-important sounds
Or dead air, then just go your rounds?
Ain't no tight-lipped, black hat can frighten us.
You high-flown, radiant types, enlighten us.

Listen, you hunks of sky, blank spaces
Absent-minded above our faces,
Between all stars, all small-time particles:
Man, beast, bird, tree, all living articles
That slump down groundward, dead and rotten,
Fly off in you and get forgotten.
Save something wunst. Get this thing solved.
Vast tracts of nothing, get involved!

The Comedian and W. D. Search for Fulfilled Homes   22 × 30 in.

W. D.'s Blues: A Ghazal for Cock Robin

Somebody shot my bird down; somebody done him dirt;
Somebody shot my bird down; somebody done him dirt;
Hangs his head like someone scorned and feelin' hurt.

His breath won't wipe my mirror; his pulse rate just won't climb;
His breath won't wipe my mirror; his pulse rate just won't climb;
His wingbeat, heartbeat and cool, sweet songs just won't keep
      time.

Come put him on a stretcher; put him in the ward, real quick;
Come put him on a stretcher; put him in the ward, real quick;
Or put him down where the fat worms all got a bone to pick.

Through the budding greenwoods his songs once veered and
    soared,
Through the budding greenwoods his songs once veered and
    soared
Like a bosun's whistle piping Spring aboard.

Once he carried sticks up and mud to line his nest;
Once he carried sticks up and mud to line his nest;
His bill's filled full of mud now, red stains on that red breast.

Once his lovesongs echoed in every lover's throat;
Once his lovesongs echoed in every lover's throat;
They've all turned their dial now; can't recall a note.

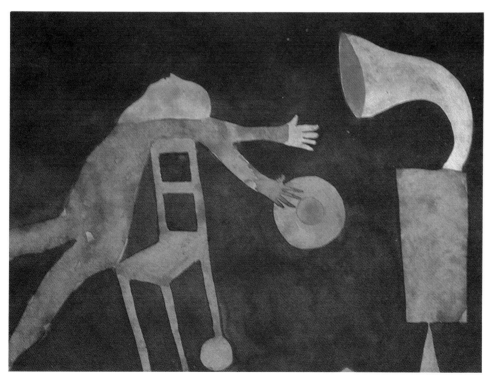

Blue Label   22 × 30 in.

Once they knew his phrasings, learned each word by heart;
Once they knew his phrasings, learned each word by heart;
His pulsebeat and his ratings slipped straight down off their
    chart.

All his friends gone hustling about their own affairs;
All his friends gone hustling about their own affairs;
Get me a weeping willow to prove somebody cares.

Ain't no one you can count on; ain't no one you can trust;
Ain't no one you can count on; ain't no one you can trust;
Gonna pack my vocal cords up and let my gonads rust.

Gonna keep one feather, 'case I ever write a song;
Gonna keep one feather, 'case I ever write a song;
Tuck it in my hatband and keep my brainwaves strong.

Gonna fly Cock Robin's feather like a bright kite in the sky;
Gonna fly Cock Robin's feather like a bright kite in the sky;
Run it up my flagpole just to keep my spirits high.

W. D. Attempts to Save Cock Robin

no sir i would not like to sell
this bird for soup yes sonnie i have heard
the polish joke and yes i know
the bird says get this joker
off my ass and indeed professor i have
seen that rembrandt with the small dog
shitting in the foreground so if you
could just inform me señor who
might own this bird or where it lives

or merely point me toward a
doctor and no fraulein kindly not
to a psychiatrist the bird
is real and heavy and the blood
gets down my neck mon capitaine but no
i am not familiar with the
napoleonic code so would you
please remove these handcuffs and
believe me no i do not have
a songbird license since quamlibet i
shot not this bird is there a
real need you behind the mask there
to lock me in this cage you see
WELL
i was practicing for
oberammergau and in this country
wood is too expensive for a cross

Coroner's Inquest

Who killed Cock Robin?
Don't you blyme me, says the sparrow;
I gone strictly straight-and-narrow,
Reformed, true-blue, a real straight arrow.
I never done that slob in.

Who saw him die?
Not I, certainly, says the fly;
My dear, this polyhedral eye
Can only make things out nearby.
I mind my own bee's wax; that's my
Alibi.

W. D. Attempts to Save Cock Robin   22 × 30 in.

Who'll wash the body?
We know too well, says the raccoon,
He sang low songs, played the buffoon
In many a road house or saloon
From bawdy midnight to high noon.
It's only fitting that so soon
He's left lowdown and cruddy.

Who'll weave his shroud?
Our local folk arts, says the spider,
Are unbecoming an outsider
Or untraditional fore-slider
Who's rejected every guide or
Guideline, led by spiritual pride or
Sensual passion through a wider
World than we're allowed.

Who'll dig his grave?
I'm committed, says the mole,
To exploring my own hole,
Liberated from control
Of any social, prefixed role;
I keep my deep molehood whole,
Seeking my true self and soul.
My blind eye's fixed on this goal;
Go find a cave.

Who'll bear his casket?
Count me out there, says the ant.
I'm too small, I simply can't.
With my legion friends, I grant
We might, yet we're all adamant
That unless he should recant
Each lewd song and surreal chant

W. D., As Sparrow, Makes Accusations   22 × 30 in.

With their sly, anarchic slant,
Even if we could we shan't
So don't ask it.

Who'll say the last words?
Of course I'd like to, says the parrot;
I'm aware that all his merit
Was so rare we can't compare it,
Yet my grief and great despair at
This sad loss, if I should share it,
Is so vast, I couldn't bear it.
Then besides, my friends don't care at
All for anyone who'd dare it.
Those that sing strange songs inherit
Faint praise—few and fast words.

        All the beasts of earth and air
          Fell a-weaselin' and a-bobbin'
        When they heard of the death
          Of poor Cock Robin.

The Ugly Little Bird

That's right; you're always blymin'
Us little birds. It's our bloomin'
  Fault whatever happens.
Huge hawks and owls does as they wants
To us small types; ain't no one wunst
  Gives them their just comeuppance.

Them high and mighty falcons, eagles,
Great albatross and nasty seagulls
  Are out there all day hustlin'.

Flamingos, herons, bleedin' parrots
Cruise around here fierce as pirates;
   But no—it's me you're hasslin'!

So what if us small birds keep naggin'
Them outsize fowls; we nicks their noggin
   And sends them packin' if
We finds one sneakin' past or snoopin'
Round our nests; why, they'd soon be snappin'
   Our nippers' heads right off!

Us little birds ain't got no choice;
We got a duty here to chase
   What invades our air spaces.
We don't mess with no artsy bards;
We just protects them baby birds,
   Replenishin' our species.

I never had no such fine feathers
Like robins got. My way's my father's:
   Feather your own nest first.
Next, you looks out for your own kind
Or you'll end up brung down and skinned
   By some big boss-bird, fast.

I got no such fine voice; I shouts:
Clear out! Then I'm off like a shot
   To liberate the skies.
I learned me one thing's half the battle:
Get you a beak like a busted bottle—
   Then go straight for the eyes.

There's some says those should get a medal
As shot him down—he made a muddle
   Of manners and strytforward meanin's.
I just says: give me real ideals,
True cheerful thoughts—none of your idle
   Moonin' about and moanin'.

The Big Beautiful Bird Has Been Shot . . .   40 × 60 in.

W. D. and Cock Robin Discuss the Dreaded Interrogation

Things such done never I've but;
Bring they can then charges what?

Their charges or the case they've built
    Won't matter. You'll still go to jail
        If you should dare plead innocent
    Since such a plea might well entail
        Some hint that they're incompetent,
Ill-willed, or covering their own guilt.
    They'll ask indefinite postponement
Of trial; meantime, *they* set your bail.

W. D. and Cock Robin Discuss the Dreaded Interrogation   41 × 30 in.

Admit must I, this like times
Commit not just did I crimes?

It's no less dangerous to plead
   Guilty as charged, asking for mercy
      From the commission or high court—
   Bound to affect your case adversely.
      You've robbed them of their favorite sport:
Dispute, time to protest or plead—
      Moreover, that cuts their fees short;
   Small wonder if they turn bloodthirsty.

         Hung get I, what matter no;
         Tongue my disengage why so?

Silence is the worst policy;
   That hints you're making some attempt
      To hide your past or guard your friends;
   Worse yet, an effort to pre-empt
      A manner sure to give offense—
That cold superiority
      On which authority depends:
   The right to hold things in contempt.

         Be possibly can hope what then,
         Me condemns defense every when?

Speak only Old High Manic-Depressive,
   South Mania or Middle Dementia;
      We'll claim errors in the translation
   Either deprive or circumvent your
      Rights under the legislation
To schizophrenia, obsessive
      Fantasies or retardation.
   They'll have to call off the whole venture.

W. D. in All Humility "Comes Clean" Concerning Cock Robin While Trying to Read Mr. Evil's (the Interrogator's) Thoughts

What could conceivably be meant
By this sly question he just asked?

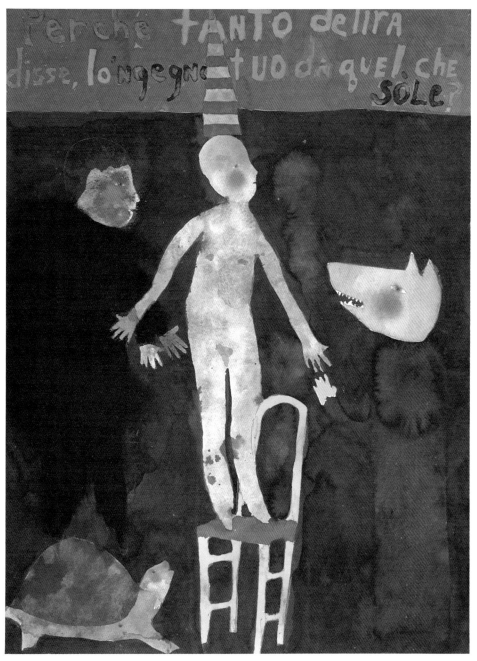

W. D. in All Humility "Comes Clean" . . .   30 × 22 in.

What could I possibly invent
    That sounds like straight, flat facts, unmasked?

I *could* confess I have this tendency
    To grow enraged at the least slight
Or, when the moon's in the ascendancy,
    To prowl through the deep woods all night

And, while there, chanced to come upon
    This long-dead body on the ground,
Or else pretend I must have gone
    Out to examine some weird sound.

I might claim that we two had grown up
    Bitter enemies since our youth;
He's bound to think someone who'd own up
    To such things, tells the whole, blunt truth.

Still, he'd not ask unless he knew
    The answer; he's just testing me.
There's nothing left for me to do
    Except admit it: "W. D."

W. D. Sits in Kafka's Chair and Is Interrogated Concerning the Assumed Death of Cock Robin

Now "W" — we'll call you "W,"
    Okay? We like the friendly touch.
Just a few questions that won't trouble you
    For long; this won't hurt much.

First: name, age, sex, race, genus,
    Specific gravity and species;
Hat size, color of hair and penis;
    Texture and frequency of faeces?

W. D. Sits in Kafka's Chair . . . 22 × 30 in.

Republican? No? Then a Baptist.
    If not, why not? If so, explain
Why you switched sides. Did your last Pap test
    Turn pink or blue? Are you insane?

When did you halt, cease, or desist
    Beating your wife? Was she friends
With this Cock Robin long? Please list
    Payments from foreign governments.

Have you changed sperm count or IQ
    Within six months? Signed a confession?
Why are we holding you? If you
    Don't know, then why ask you this question?

A simple yes or no is all
    We want; the truth always shines through.
Thank you. Please wait out in the hall
    Until somebody comes for you.

W. D., without Disguise, Is Recognized by the Dark Comedian but Denies His Relationship with Cock Robin

"Perhaps you could enlighten us:
    Just where did this Cock Robin dwell?"
    That would be difficult to tell.
(Difficult. Also hazardous.)

"You never visited his garden?"
    Can't say I've ever met the chap.
    (Whoever said he had, you'd clap
In irons beyond parole or pardon.)

"Then you were not his follower?"
    Not so much as you could notice.
    (Not you—stone blind! Look, your scapegoat is
Escaping from your grasp, dear sir.)

I stonewalled like a rock, came through
Unscathed, yet only said what's true.
I made them all look bad, then flew
Their coop. What kind of bird just crew?

W. D., without Disguise, Is Recognized   22 × 30 in.

Credo

—For Antonia Quintana Pigno

This is the song
Cock Robin sung.

This is the breath, forthright and strong,
That lifted the steady, airborne song
Cock Robin sung.

This is the lung, the throat, the tongue,
That moved the breath, forthright and strong,

Supporting the steady, airborne song
Cock Robin sung.

These are the breezes, east and west,
That swelled the lung, the throat, the tongue,
That shaped the breath, forthright and strong,
Lofting the steady, airborne song
Cock Robin sung.

This is the 8-storey-high birds' nest
Blown by the breezes, east and west,
That wakened the lung, the throat, the tongue,
To craft the breath, forthright and strong,
Bearing along the airborne song
Cock Robin sung.

This is the worm, a creeping pest,
That found the 8-storey-tall birds' nest
Rocked by breezes to east and west
That stirred the lung, the throat, the tongue,
To fashion the breath, forthright and strong,
And waft along the airborne song
Cock Robin sung.

This is the rumor, slimy and sly,
That crept like worms or a crawling pest
Around the 8-storey roost or nest
Swung by the breezes to east and to west,
Driving the lung, the throat, the tongue,
To channel the breath, forthright and strong,
Buoying along the airborne song
Cock Robin sung.

Here's old Mr. Evil who told the lie
That started the rumor, smirking and sly,
Spreading like worms or a creeping pest
Surrounding the 8-storey perch or nest

Tilting as breezes blew, east or west,
Impelling the lung, the throat, the tongue,
To manage the breath, forthright and strong,
And carry along the airborne song
Cock Robin sung.

These are dark angels who fly up and spy
Where old Mr. Evil's telling his lie
That fathered the rumor, slippery and sly,
Bristling like worms, some plague or pest,
That climbed the 8-storey tower or nest
Leaning as breezes blew east, blew west,
Inflating the lung, the throat, the tongue,
To master the breath, forthright and strong,
And spirit along the airborne song
Cock Robin sung.

Here are pink putti who dogfight the sky
Against the dark angels that fly past and spy
Then pecked Mr. Evil for telling that lie,
Checked the vile rumor, insidious and sly,
And fed on the worms, the plump, white pest
That gnawed at the 8-storey aerie or nest
Lurching as breezes blew east and west,
Inspiring the lung, the throat, the tongue
To pilot the breath, forthright and strong,
And draft on its thermals the airborne song
Cock Robin sung.

Here is the void, the blank, black eye
That watches pink putti dogfight the sky
To harry dark angels that fly high to spy
While old Mr. Evil's still telling his lie,
And on creeps the rumor, sinuous, sly,
Like worms into hiding or some unknown pest
That could riddle the 8-storey towering nest
Battered by breezes from east and from west,

Empowering the breath, forthright and strong,
That saved so long from rot and from wrong
The lifelong, lovesprung, airborne song
Cock Robin sung.

W. D. in Early Morning Contemplates . . .   30 × 22 in.

W. D. Creates a Device for Escaping

After one first green step ahead
I brake down on this foot of red
    A stop foot, then a go foot

One arm, one leg in my own spokes
A balance wheel of counterstrokes
    A to foot, then a fro foot

These blood-red hands before my face
Carrots that keep me at my pace
    A fast foot, then a slow foot

W. D. Creates a Device for Escaping   22 × 30 in.

As a pit pony cranks a winch
Ixion axles, inch by inch
    A start foot, then a whoa foot

Beneath the circling stars and seasons
Time's roulette game of rhymes and reasons
    A con foot, then a pro foot

Plodding, wing-burdened like a pack
This dead-weight Robin on my back
    A heel foot, then a toe foot

He wears my stripes, he rides my wheel
How shall my galls and blisters heal?
    A high foot, then a low foot

And where do ten-ton Robins sleep?
On my back still while I still creep
    A quid foot, then a quo foot

I could cut loose, leaving him bound
To ride this giddy Fun-Go-Round
    A joy foot, then a woe foot

Or turn weak like old Sisyface
Letting him roll back to the base
    A yes foot, then a no foot.

Disguised as Cook Robin, W. D. Escapes

Come, Rosie Angel, faced with blues,
  Join hands and we'll be piped together
    Pilots of our own quarter, decked
In multiplicity's fast hues—

This Joseph's cloak that many a feather
    Weaves—in fact, a factory reject

That is becoming without seems.
    Fortuna's game wheel be our helm;
      We'll shoot the jazzy straits of I-Am,
Flee all Utopia's bonded schemes
    Of ideal bondage for a live realm
      Where I'll lush up my lute like Khayyam

While you beside me, blushing warm,
    Sing out like Saki. At this wheel
      We'll steer, veer, chart what course we shipped,
Skipped, slipped out, then rode out the storm
    Reeling our catch of all that *is* real
      Out of this land of Gyp and Be Gypped.

Disguised as Cock Robin, W. D. Escapes   22 × 30 in.

Assuming Fine Feathers, W. D. Takes Flight

Over these cheekbones,
  Streaked thick with bristle,
Draw down the soft down
  Sleek as a whistle.
    See feedle, seedle, tweedle tree.

My slimy nostrils,
  My slithery lips
Turn to a beak, blunt
  As dry facts or tinsnips.
    Homo nonsapiens conturbat me.

These split lids fit
  My eye like a filter;
The dim world clicks
  To a new green kilter.
    Earclay, eanseclay ymay ightsay.

Scapular, spellbound,
  These feathers drape
My shoulderblades
  Like an opera cape
    Cheggange meggee; freggee meggee.

Or a Sioux priest's vestments;
  Dare to assume
The adept's full mantle
  And the long tail-plume.
    Sing-a-ling, wing-wary-way.

Through clouds of unknowing
  I veer and sail;

W. D. Intuitively Dismisses the Charges   41 × 30 in.

Below, men's heads
   And dogs' heads wail—
      In nubibus, ignotum per ignotius—

Hot on my track still,
   But I tricked 'em;
Now who's your criminal;
   Where's your victim?
      Dee-flee-a-beadle-tweedle-free!

W. D. Disguised as Cock Robin and Hidden Deep in Crimson

They'll never find me hidden
So close to them, inside
Switched-on electric wires
Or nerve ends, in forbidden
Urges, rage, lust, pride,
Sweet murderous desires,
The medulla of old fires.

I go cloaked in the charged rag
That matadors must wave
To keep them out of sight;
Protected by the flag
They run up in the brave
Country of Dynamite;
I lurk in the Geistzeit.

I ride the pulse that swells
Lips, nails, all feverish parts;
I wear the blushing scarlet
Alphabet that spells
The blazing braille of hearts,

The shorted shorts of the harlot,
Virgin, housewife, starlet.

I dopplegang some grander
Land that schizophrenics
Colonize from earth,
One with the salamander,
With that flaming phoenix
Or lodgepole pine whose clenched cones need
The forest fire to cast their seed.

Auction

For the gay tailfeathers, say, what'll you pay?—
Red, blue and purple plumes—a bouquet
Of heather-spume or a lit fountain's spray. Hey!
Shave a fine penpoint, whisk dusk away
Or trim sharp the virginals' quills when you play.

Who'll buy an eye—aye, buy an eye!
This ringset onyx jet, black tack for your tie
Or oldtimer's photocell, spy in the sky,
Laserbeam click-ticking off who's slipped by
Or to glow soft by the cribside till dawntide draws nigh.

What am I bid for this swift wing?—
A deft wing, an arched-out lifting thing
To nail fast on your hallwalls or set fling
The soul's boomerang, the young shepherd's sling
That brings huge despair down, crowns the new king.

How much for the bones?—built-light-for-flight bones,
Leached, bleached out, scaled to high kite zones—
Buoyance that scoured out, scored, then bored right, loans

W. D. Disguised as Cock Robin . . . 30 × 22 in.

Range to a flute floating out warm and bright tones
Over the vast frozen waste no man owns.

How far will you go for his hard, sharp toenails?—
For harp picks, guitar picks, to pick locks, open jails,
Thumb tacks, phononeedles, needles to sew sails,
To turn toward true North in high snowthrown trails
Or seek the soft South when winter winds blow gales.

For this heart, smart and artful, where will you start?
A life's thump pump, formed to pyrite love's feverchart!
Let's throw in lights, liver, lungs, each left, torn apart,
Worn out part. Who'll start out—shebang and applecart
Go along; so what's wrong? Who'll buy a heart?

> I, said the fly, I go for the eye.
> Me, said the beetle, I'll buy me a bone.
> Mine, said the earthworm, I take the heart.

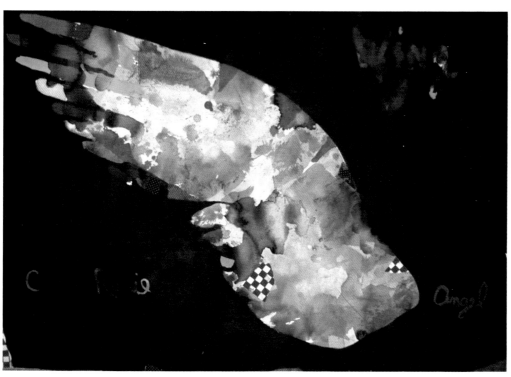

Auction   30 × 41 in.

Afterword
How Is A Poem Like A Picture?
The Art(s) of W. D. Snodgrass And DeLoss McGraw

The Roman poet Horace, in his *Ars Poetica*, did not mean to stir the waters extravagantly when he gave the phrase "ut pictura poesis" to the world. He said only that

> A poem is like a picture: one strikes your fancy more, the nearer you stand; another, the farther away. This courts the shade, that will wish to be seen in the light, and dreads not the critic insight of the judge. This pleased but once; that, though ten times called for, will always please.

Horace appreciated the happy similarity of some things in a picture to some things in a poem; he suggested, mildly, that enjoyment of a good painting is like enjoyment of a good poem. Later commentators, particularly in the Renaissance, took matters more seriously and made much of these similarities, doing so, it now seems, to enhance the prestige and importance of painting, an art not then accorded the dignity of poetry. Thus we may read John Dryden's translation and endorsement of Charles du Fresnoy's declaration that "Painting and Poesy are two sisters, which are so like in all things, that they mutually lend to each other, both their name and office. One is called a dumb poesy, and the other a speaking picture." Here is the notion that the two arts may help each other.

The possibility of such symbiosis, however, is exactly what G. E. Lessing attacked in his enormously influential treatise *Laokoön* (1766). Lessing suggested that Horace's linkage of the two arts was no more than a happy figure of speech. The ancients, he said, really knew that painting and poetry differed both in the means they employed and in the objects of their attention. Painting was concerned with the representation of objects in space. Poetry was concerned with the narration of progressive actions. For the one art, dimension and description were essential; for the other, time and events were what counted.

This strong disagreement about the relationship of the two arts has been carried out on the level of theory for centuries—Lessing has disagreed with Horace and many commentators have, in turn, disagreed with Lessing. Meanwhile, the artists themselves have simply ignored the controversy and have struck up conspiracies to resolve their apparent differences and to unite their energies. As the Lessings argue, the William Blakes arrive to demonstrate that copper etchings and celestial poetry may fit on the same page, worked by the same hand, praising the same god—each art impoverished, if not rendered impossible, without the other. Charles Dickens found it useful to combine his sketches of London life and Parliament with his prose descriptions of those subjects; he brought the two together in *Sketches by Boz.* Lewis Carroll called on Sir John Tenniel to provide illustrative life for *Alice in Wonderland* and *The Hunting of the Snark.* D. H. Lawrence painted as he wrote. And Franz Kafka distributed line drawings in the texts of his horrific accounts of men dwarfed and humiliated by events; he seemed to think they added further sprightliness to his humor. In Kafka, no one can say what is "action" and what is "description."

These assorted examples reveal the continual erosion of the artificial barriers of definition between the arts. If Walter Pater was right to claim that "all art constantly aspires towards the condition of music," an even more justifiable claim would be that none of the arts is a separate, inviolable province. Each seems open to the other; they all "tend" to the "condition" of the other. Ezra Pound joins forces with Constantin Brancusi and Henri-Gaudier Brzeska in order to define the unique power of artistic "modernity"; W. B. Yeats, former art student, meditates on watercolors and sketches before writing "On a Picture of a Black Centaur by Edmund Dulac"; W. H. Auden collaborates with Igor Stravinsky to produce *The Rake's Progress;* Sidney Nolan unites with Robert Lowell to make *Near the Ocean;* John Ashbery, Kenneth Koch, James Schuyler, and Frank O'Hara become "the New York poets" of the 1960s by first looking to the paintings of Jackson Pollack, Franz Kline, and Willem de Kooning. The energy of art speaks a common language; it need not be broken into inaccessible dialects.

Yet many artists begin alone, trusting nothing but their own impulses, the rhythms in which they are first comfortable. Only with maturity and experience do they come by the knowledge and the pleasure of how the self can be expanded through the incorporation of new modes of expression. In the career of W. D. Snodgrass, for instance, what began in the 1950s as a painfully intense scrutiny of the singular self has now (in the 1970s and 1980s) become the depiction of a crowded landscape of multiple selves, characters in opposition—the many rather than the one. In *Heart's Needle* (1959), his first book of poems, "Snodgrass is walking through the universe" but is doing so, make no mistake about it, *alone.* When he remarks in that volume that "I carry a scared silence / with me like my smell," he reveals an essential truth about the narrow conventions in which he was writing at the time. The vogue of "confessional poetry" inaugurated by *Heart's Needle* (and, to a lesser extent, by Robert Lowell's *Life Studies*) drew exclusively on the singularity of one speaker; it spoke of the ravages of *his* existence and suggested that the rest of life was mere background to that tragedy.

But Snodgrass did not remain in the small room of confessional poetry. Moving beyond the claustrophobia of selfhood, Snodgrass published *After Experience* (1968) and thereby gave notice both to himself and his readers that he had achieved considerable distance from personal travail. He was now prepared to explore terrain that was unfamiliar because it was not of his own making. Poems about his daughter, about his failing marriage, about the dislocations of his academic existence, make up but part of the volume. The voice of fragility and vulnerability is still present. But poems like "Planting a Magnolia" announce that Snodgrass is no longer speaking about his own puniness, but about human puniness in general. The planted tree represents all those forces superior in strength to the strength of humankind; it is not the poet alone who is insignificant when compared to the "mystery" and the "obscene blunt beauty" of that tree. Hence the use of the first-person *plural* pronoun: it is "we" who are belittled by the presence of the magnolia and its ancient roots, and it is "we" who will die before the tree does.

But the real departures in *After Experience* do not come with the new positions Snodgrass can assume in the face of his weakness and the superior force of the universe, but with his discovery of an art form not his own: painting. Owing to a series of pedagogical accidents, the poet is suddenly made to confront Matisse, Monet, Vuillard, Manet, and Van Gogh. And, with that confrontation, the sensibility and the art of the poet undergo an extraordinary change. One art, "tending" toward another, is transformed.

Snodgrass's essay about the discovery of the five painters and their paintings, "Poems about Paintings," reveals the seductive power possessed by something beyond him and other than him. Talking about Claude Monet's "Les Nymphéas," he says:

> Sitting before it for long hours at the museum, I often had the sensation that if I did not get up and leave the room, the guards might well come in and find me missing. . . . I, trying to absorb this picture—might be absorbed by it.

Such fear of disappearance was, in turn, connected with another sensation provided by the painting—the sensation of liberation. "Les Nymphéas" was for Snodgrass "about the effort to break down the armoring of the self and its beliefs and ideas; one might become an energy among energies, open to the flux of experience, absorbing and being absorbed by sensation." These profound alterations in Snodgrass's way of looking at himself and at the world, alterations caused by the impact of another form of art on his own, are summed up by his recognition that the five paintings all involved a theme—incarceration and liberation—that he now knew was central to his development as a poet: "an extremely ambivalent feeling toward a womblike containment: on the one hand a fierce desire to escape; on the other, a desire to be captured and contained."

That recognition changed Snodgrass as a poet. And it illustrates the great power the forms and expressions of one art can have on those of another. After the five "poems about paintings" in *After Experience*, Snodgrass moved to a more active involvement with the problems of translation (translation itself being a departure from selfhood into the sensibility of another). Then, in *The Führer Bunker: A Cycle of Poems in Progress* (1977), he moved to an imaginative recreation of an entire chorus of tortured voices, each with its own inflections, accent, and willfulness. *The Führer Bunker* is, in fact, about the power of will and the associated power of individual autonomy, themes close to Snodgrass all his career, but now enacted by characters drawn out of the darkest and most disturbed pages of this century's history. In a singularly ambitious demonstration of the artistic facility John Keats called "negative capability," Snodgrass lets his own mind and imagination drift free so that he can enter the driven and poisoned minds of Adolf Hitler and those close to him in the final days of the Third Reich. Rant, song, dream and nightmare, proclamation, and idle talk—all fill the page as they fill the reader's mind. The diversity of the individuals present in the bunker is made manifest by the range of poetic forms selected for them: everything from couplet to villanelle. And lurking behind all the presences is the mind of Hitler: total will imprisoned by absolute obsession.

After the dark world of *The Führer Bunker*, Snodgrass has moved to a world quite different, a world seemingly lighter and more playful in tone, a world whose music and rhythm are supplied by a nursery rhyme, a fabulous world of animals and birds. And, most interesting to anyone tracing Snodgrass's career, this transformation has come directly from the power of a painter: DeLoss McGraw.

Perhaps the first observation to be made about the impact of McGraw on Snodgrass's work is that the painter proved to be an excellent reader of poetry and showed that the poet in time could become an excellent reader of visual creations. In first writing to Snodgrass in 1982, McGraw said that he had seen a "childlike attitude toward death" in the poet's work. That perception, the kind of insight between two artists that Nathaniel Hawthorne once called "the shock of recognition," was the beginning of the shared understanding that was later to unite the work of the two men.

The Death of Cock Robin, the result of that union, wholly fuses the energies of two artists. It is not paintings "about" poems any more than it is poems about certain paintings. It is instead the product of one artist (whether painter or poet) enlivened and strengthened by the work of another (the painter, forty years of age, and the poet, some twenty years older, become exact contemporaries in that fusion). Neither artist nor art takes the upper hand in this relationship, for each of them gets to see ways in which the limitations of his art can be pushed back and opened up. And each artist reserves the right, an ultimate privilege, of *mis*reading the work of the other. Snodgrass has said, "We both often find that we've misunderstood each other," but he adds, "Those misreadings nearly always prove fertile."

The ground on which the poet and the painter have found themselves is the buried past of childhood. The vehicle of their artistic association is a childish rhyme, "The Death of Cock Robin," about the death of an innocent. Like many such rhymes, its apparent naïveté disguises the violence and pain residing beneath the surface of the story. In the world of nursery rhymes trauma is anesthetized by simple verbal beats and syncopation, thus revealing the wonderful power of children to assimilate pain by giving it pattern and making it playful.

The nursery rhyme "Cock Robin," ostensibly about the regrettable death of a bird, is in fact about the complicity of many living things in the world of death. The sparrow has killed the robin, and everyone else, from beetle to owl to dove, thrush, and bull, seems glad to play a part in all the traditional rites—from mourning to burial. For that reason, the rhyme gained popularity in the mid-eighteenth century as an Aesopian way of explaining the fall of Robert Walpole's ministry under George III of England. It became, then, a rhyme about intrigue and deceit.

And that is the very subject of the paintings/poems titled *The Death of Cock Robin.* Like the nursery rhyme, this unified work feigns jocularity to focus on the dark business of interrogation, accusation, betrayal, and intrigue. The noxious smell of complicity is everywhere. The poem begins with "charges," it portrays fear and persecution, and it ends with death. Cock Robin is the victim of forces moving implacably against him. Unlike the nursery rhyme, however, the work includes a character who is part friend to Cock Robin, part his alter ego, and part witness to his destruction. That character is "W. D.," whose name, interestingly enough, happens not to have been the invention of the poet, but of the painter. "W. D." comforts Cock Robin and provides him safe haven while he studies the plight faced by the bird. More thoughtful and analytical than Cock Robin, "W. D." is at once the creation of the painter and the voice of the poet, the voice of anyone who, looking on pain and defeat, asks for help and for explanation. "W. D.," then, is *us* as we read the poem. It is the device used by the painter and the poet to lure us into their joint enterprise and its drama.

But the power of that enterprise does not issue from just this device. Rather, the poems, limited by their confinement in words, crucially depend on the way they become defined and expanded by the work of DeLoss McGraw. By the same token, McGraw's work, confined in shape and color, becomes defined and "voiced" by its relationship to those poems. The wonder of the relationship is that it is perfectly reciprocal; artist answers to artist, each provoking, surprising, and challenging the other. The paintings are thus organically a part of *The Death of Cock Robin* and not at all its "illustration."

Look, for instance, at the painting/poem titled "W. D. and Cock Robin Discuss the Dreaded Interrogation." To read this work correctly, one must appreciate the fact that the lines given to "W. D." make more sense when read backward than when read forward; this contraposition is made vivid by the fact that the painting sees "W. D." as upside-down, the very figure of contrariness. Or look at the painting/poem titled "Cock Robin's Roost Protects W. D. From Mr. Evil," in which the acrostic nature of the poem is replicated by the visual quality of Cock Robin's roost, which functions as a barrier separating "W. D." from "Mr. Evil."

McGraw's work is large, bold, and assertive and his paintings, as these examples and others demonstrate, invest the collective work with the energy, absurdity, childishness, and stark horror of Cock Robin's persecution and death. His colors fill the eye; his shapes are at times massive but at other times tiny and delicate. His range enables him to convey a sense both of the gigantic forces bearing down on Cock Robin and of the fragility of the world he inhabits. McGraw is also a whimsical painter, his vision revealing that he knows there is a kind of desperate lunacy in the struggle he places before us. Like Franz Kafka, McGraw seems to understand the macabre humor of the universe: that it is without equity and fairness but is filled with much surprise, commotion, and even beauty. McGraw is the kind of artist who would understand the truth of a statement James Joyce once made in a letter to his son:

"For more than fifty years my eyes have stared at nullity, where they have found a beautiful nothing." McGraw and Joyce both perceive the astonishing and complex beauty of the world, even while comprehending that such a world might be devoid of meaning.

From their partnership, Snodgrass and McGraw say to those who see and read their work that the annihilation stored up for Cock Robin—and indeed for all of us—will hardly be bleak. It will be filled with animation, color, song, and some good company. The vision the painter and the poet share is revealed in, for instance, "W. D. Assists in the Protection of Cock Robin's Roost," where W. D.'s solicitude is represented by his plural selves floating and working everywhere in the air. There is no sense in either the poem or the painting of loneliness or despair but rather splendid flashes of energy and dynamic determination. Look, for example, at "W. D. Picks a Bouquet for Cock Robin but Cannot Separate the Thorns from the Flowers" (many of the paintings sharing titles with poems came first from the inspiration of the painter, not from the poet). Here the tone of McGraw's work, surprisingly enough, is placid. Instead of the isolated despair of introspection, a genuine stability and poise in color and design and in rhyme scheme predominate. The painter and the poet seem vigorously involved in an effort to repudiate depression by euphoria, ruination by construction. Theirs is that most admirable and rare of creations: a joint project in the artistic resurrection of the human spirit.

For DeLoss McGraw, such alliance is the very stuff of an artistic life. In his paintings and watercolors McGraw previously turned to the work of the Anglo-Irish poet W. B. Yeats and imagined a kind of cooperative effort with Yeats that abridges the decades. McGraw has also imagined the elements of creation, emotion, and thought infusing some of Yeats's greatest moments as a poet and has reproduced those elements in his own medium. The result is a commentary on those poems that is as rich as much verbal analysis. McGraw has also been fascinated by the great myth of transformation and superhuman power found in the story of Frankenstein's creature: in responding to the work of a young poet, Bart Thurber, he painted a series of vivid watercolors called *Frankenstein and Mary Shelley* (1984).

From his mother, a teacher in Oklahoma, McGraw learned the truth of poetic language and, as a very young man, felt compelled to put down in line and color the themes that he knew inhered in words but could for him be imagined only graphically. He has dedicated much of his career to refuting the notion that the arts are necessarily isolated from one another. Indeed, as McGraw has gone about the business of assimilating the literary and making it serve the interests of the pictorial, he has overcome a taboo fashionable in this time, namely that painters may only at their peril become "literary." When he was first inspired to write to W. D. Snodgrass, McGraw inquired if he could use the poet's name in a pair of color lithographs—"W. D. Snodgrass, You Sentimental Fool" and "W. D. Snodgrass, You Silly Man, Come in Out of the Storm." In coming to work more closely with Snodgrass thereafter, in maintaining a vigorous correspondence with him, and in seeing how a practicing poet has developed, McGraw has been able to imagine ways of providing the visual complement to Snodgrass's lexical and rhythmic achievements. The result, open to the eye and mind, is an enormously handsome fusion of the best work of two practiced and original artists. Our eyes and minds are strengthened in encountering that work, and we are in the presence of a triumphant doubling of creative power.

William M. Chace
English Department of Stanford University

Owners and Locations of the Paintings
(Photography Courtesy of Harcourts Contemporary,
San Francisco)

Mr. and Mrs. Paul Aberly, Bloomfield Hills, Michigan
W. D. Assists in the Protection of Cock Robin's Roost
W. D. Consults with Kafka and Dostoevski Concerning the
Whereabouts of Cock Robin

Robert and Kiki Ballard, San Francisco, California
Lullaby: The Comforting of Cock Robin

Donald and Jessica Block, Lafayette, California
W. D. Sits in Kafka's Chair and Is Interrogated Concerning the
Assumed Death of Cock Robin

Paul Bruggemans, Beverly Hills, California
Blue Label

Mr. and Mrs. Stacy Couture, Kettleman, California
Cock Robin's Roost Protects W. D. from Mr. Evil

R. B. Dicker, Sydney, Australia
W. D. Becomes Entangled in the Nest of His Thought

Dr. Keith A. Fair, Fremont, California
W. D. Is Concerned about the Character Assassination of Cock Robin

Jack and Connie Glenn, Long Beach, California
W. D., without Disguise, Is Recognized by the Dark Comedian but
Denies His Relationship with Cock Robin

D. J. Hales, Palo Alto, California
W. D. Creates a Device for Escaping

Grant and Mary Holcomb, Rochester, New York
The Poet Ridiculed by Hysterical Academics

Stephane Janssen, Beverly Hills, California
Cock Robin Takes Refuge in the Storm House
Disguised as Cock Robin, W. D. Escapes
W. D., as Sparrow, Makes Accusations
W. D. Attempts to Save Cock Robin
W. D. Finds Cock Robin
W. D. Disguised as Cock Robin and Hidden Deep in Crimson

Drs. Harvey and Ann Kershner, Santa Ana, California
W. D. Lifts Ten Times the Weight of His Own Body

Robert McDonald, San Francisco, California
W. D. Intuitively Dismisses the Charges

Shannon McGraw, San Diego, California
W. D. in Early Morning Contemplates the Qualities of Cock Robin—
after Giotto

Midwestern University, Wichita Falls, Texas
W. D. in All Humility "Comes Clean" Concerning Cock Robin While
Trying to Read Mr. Evil's (the Interrogator's) Thoughts

Private Collection
Auction
The Big Beautiful Bird Has Been Shot by the Ugly Little Bird
Cock Robin Consults with His Storm Family
The Comedian and W. D. Search for Fulfilled Homes
W. D. Assists in Supporting Cock Robin's Nest (Saratoga,
California)
W. D. and Cock Robin Discuss the Dreaded Interrogation
W. D., Don't Fear That Animal (Seattle, Washington)
W. D. Picks a Bouquet for Cock Robin but Cannot Separate the Thorns
from the Flowers
W. D. Searches for Cock Robin in the Weave of His Thought
W. D. Tries to Warn Cock Robin (Saratoga, California)

W. D. and Kathleen Snodgrass, Newark, Delaware
W. D. Creates a Device for Inverting Mr. Evil

George and Adrienne Weir, Escondido, California
W. D. Escapes the Dream (jacket illustration)

Kent C. Wilson, Danville, California
W. D. Meets Mr. Evil While Removing the Record of Bartok and Replacing It with a Recent Recording by the Everly Brothers in Order to Create a Mood Conducive to Searching for Cock Robin (first version)